TAPES
IN DRAG:
POETRY &
REMORSE

LVF.LVX

Title: Tapes in Drag: Poetry & Remorse
Author: LVF LVX
Publisher: MallMagick
Print Publication Date: June 2024
First Edition Paperback

ISBN Paperback 979-8-9908212-0-0

Description: Inspired by the works of Rainer Maria Rilke and
Rumi, *Tapes in Drag: Poetry & Remorse*, LVF.LVX presents a
poetic-memoir that recounts love, loss–*or at least*– a love that
never was. By delving into her own vulnerability, she comes to
experience the power of unrealized fears, drawing from the
ethereal to transcend beauty from grief.

Keywords: poetry, love poems, esotericism, mysticism, occult,
metaphysics, literature and fiction, women authors, relationships,
heartbreak, love & loss, grief, self-discovery, introspective,
inspiration, healing

Printed in the United States of America

Visit us at MallMagick.com

To my Beloved,
At last, I am free.

Acknowledgements

This collection is an homage to my very first, now-defunct blog, *Tapes in Drag* (https://tapesindrag.blogspot.com); an archive of originally published pieces and the first of my poetic memoirs.

The poems: "a billion years from now" (then, published as "Seeing You") and the original version of "Aletheia" were published in Brandeis University's *Laurel Moon Literary Magazine* in 2015.

Contents

CHAPTER TWO: LOSS

CHAPTER THREE: EPIPHANY

Prologue

What you are about to read is all very real.

They are relationships, moments of love, anger, sorrow, and ecstasy; initiations, visions, and the inner workings of an individual who wanted nothing more than to love and be loved.

They are symphonies and myths, symbols and languages, messages from muses, and frequencies from the ethers. They are poems that I wrote over a decade ago, having served as an escape from the traumas and grieving I experienced when I felt all hope was gone.

It wasn't.

Soon after I closed that chapter of my life, I had seemingly forgotten all about them; forgotten who I was and where I was going. For years, I had abandoned the very essence that makes me who I am and who I will become. I never intended to forget, but life had a way of overshadowing my purpose—at least, until I was ready for it.

It wasn't until recently, when I came across my old notebooks, blog, and boxes full of old tapes, that the memories alongside them—the highs and lows of an era—came flooding back. It felt like lifetimes ago. And perhaps they were.

These poems speak of a young heart, blissfully open and unaware of the love and unrealized fears she possessed and that laid dormant within her. She describes both the beauty and trials of such a pure encounter only to realize that life has a will of its own. We experience life through a secret series of initiations: "*to make the unconscious conscious,*" said the great, Carl Jung. With enough awareness, she begins to notice the world is a reflection of her heart and psyche, both avowedly at odds. She mirrors and is a mirror of the world.

Tapes in Drag: Poetry & Remorse is more than mere poetry, performance, or ritual. It is medium and music simultaneously being dragged into a distorted cacophony: the sound of life moving beyond your control. It is the wail and last words of a daemon manifesting through audio tape—its music struggling to be heard. Essentially, it is the sacrificial offering of a song in exchange for alchemical irony.

You have arrived at the first initiation.

Alas, the unraveling.

CHAPTER
ONE
LOVE

I. a billion years from now

i could hear this song a thousand times.
a thousand years from now,
i'll be someone else completely.

i watched you from the rooftop
like the tallest light post
that just stands still.
you couldn't see me.
it was dark and
i was somewhere up above you.

>   *was i god,*
>   *or a sniper?*

my perspective reaches farther than
            all your daily routes.
i came by like a breeze barely noticed—
nudity underneath one's clothing
things that are always there but unseen,
like time and all the fragments that
pull us together and back apart again.
only to draw us into collision.

>   i'll be Andromeda,
>   jumping into the arms
>   of the Milky Way Galaxy.

II. karmic lover

your lips are perfect.
warm touch,
sensuality
all over.

i love that you're just like me.
a guy version,
but tall.

you wrote my name on your tongue,
tattooed my heart on your sleeve.
gave each other something to smile about
before heading back home to our wives.

i once had a husband.

i know how it feels to be
oh, so comfortable...
resisting change
when change is everything.

passion-filled whirlwind of emotion envelops,
stirring up your space inside.

you smirk because you're happy.
i know because i'm happiest with you.

i'll leave it there if i have to.
hang it on the wall
just to look at it
every so often.

III. in waves

yesterday's memories wash ashore
like today's dreams at a harbor.
they crash unto my being like
hard, slapping
waves of reality
that move me to the core,
penetrating
my soul
like an astral projection.

i see you're really good at that.

IV. just a dream

i countdown from ten.
still hypnotized.

i'm floating above the waters.
where the ocean meets the sun;
where the sun meets the land.

it was sundown and the sky was pink.
you gave me away to yourself
in a dream.

we woke up happy.

V. wills

there you were...

the work of a cosmic conspiracy.

a higher form of magick that is beyond me.

i hesitate for a moment
            before i walk into
            the co-creation dream.

i'm always unsure.
            we
            are always unsure.

our wills,
they have a mind of their own.

we manifest one another
            but nothing ever changes,
            we still can't face each other.

our consciousness is chaotic.
            you are my desire and fear incarnate.
            my dream and my shadow.

i'm getting to know you
on a different level now.
you're closer to me than ever
            pretending to be strangers.

VI. gammas

it's sometimes difficult,
　　　　stalled by time and space—

　　　　　a tantric dance
　　　　　fueled by
　　　　　the same but opposite natures

learning the virtues of patience and strength,

　　　　　the meaning of true love.

it's a passion that creates gammas.
　　　　it's that look in your eyes.

i want to jump in there and kiss you.
　　　　let the stars read our story.

VII. to my other

un/divided soul,

you seem unaware
of the blueprint you speak;
the thoughts in your mind that
haunt you in sleep—
the stars that guide you
back to yourself;
the love you long for,
once held.

she showers in rose petals
waiting for the day
you remember a promise
that shatters the physical,
time and space,
and all imaginary distance
we've created in our

sick,

sick

minds.

VIII. echoes

i cast you out to sea
for that pearl in your eyes.
it's lost somewhere
between the depths and the skies.
it's got my promise on it.

> your promise is my veil,
> recalling your love
> like an echo around my finger.

IX. abandonment issues

i love
that which moves me,
makes me feel,
and shakes me to the core...
even if just a little.

X. your eyes are a well

no matter how much you try to

fool me / fool you,

your eyes give it away.

they sing

tiny daggers through my heart.

      joy.

      slasher-massacre.

reminding me of how awesome it is
to feel that way again.

no more violence for dreams,
your presence disarms me.

your song,

like creeping death at the bottom of a wishing well

found its way to me

just before your last breath.

      just before my last ...

CHAPTER
TWO
LOSS

I. songs of sleep

you came suddenly,
like a fork splitting a one-way road.

   shit.

i can't tell which path i'm on.

   can you see me?

it was as if i walked into a mirror.
the glass shatters.
cuts my finger.

i'm alright.
i live.

my bleeding is a personal ritual and reminder of my
being human.
we've both admitted to our addictions.

the mirror is personified.

yes, it has a name.
i've been trying to figure it out.
again, i can't sleep at night.
i'm excited about tomorrow.

   what is tomorrow?
   are you there tomorrow?
   are you me,
   still?

fragmented into a million pieces,
the light reflects off broken glass.

i can see now.

<have we been swallowed by the labyrinth?
the illusion of our divided being?>

you seem to be fine, in a strange way.

we've returned to our broken homes:
those planets in
complete misunderstanding.

but is that not the easy way out?
isn't that the antithesis of our purpose?

<< let's stick to what we know >>

yea.

<< don't listen to her.
don't pay any attention to that moon inside of you that
speaks to you in dreams and reminds you which way is
up. >>

it would be far too drastic to step into
that part of yourself that sings you to
sleep and wishes you weren't such a
stranger.

II. sweet dreams

the best dreams at night
destroy you in the morning.

III. i met a beast

stared into the corner of dawn.
i see
a beautiful beast—
serene,
like unmoved water.
i want to touch it
to find a moving stillness.

i feel more alive than ever
            in this half-asleep dream.
i get closer,
but it's all changed.

your once majestic face
expands like a frilled neck lizard—
snapping,
with claws for teeth.
chirps of furious insecurities,
shaking,
like a pubescent boy,
vomiting his inner rage.

rays of the sun
shining on me,
            shining on you.
exposing what you are:

brilliant hate

            embodied as my love.

IV. no one ever knows anyone

its effects are going away now...

happy dopamine.
serotonin loves me with a blindfold on.

ecstasy in my arms
is the surface of things.

kama sutra with potential
only i see.

you think you know me,
but i am in skin.

inside my chest
is
            more passion than anything
            you've ever known.

there's a stranger
beating—
tearing down your affair with my persona.

        you're on a comfortable high.

it's an overload
of new memories,
never ending futures,
            and worlds that don't exist,

with eyes purer than
virginity itself.

a chastity belt around your deepest thoughts.
we have the same taste in movies.

a mother-father god and
Nietzsche's 'no-need-for-relationship'
            are my pillow.
it will save me from things harder to let go of
than the grip keeping me from falling 20 stories high.

i'm coming down now,
on my own
before i meet the ground
faster than i met you.

you're welcome to join me
in a bed deep inside her
penetrating within her
            soul
            that meets the core.

if we make it,
we will be what we once were
            without the expectations of the drug,
            without pretending
like we know each other.

i'll give us the chance to do so.

V. vague poem

<<**REDACTED**>>

i wrote a vague poem
to tie around my finger;
a secret meal
like a one time birthday wish.

VI. love and loss

when two worlds overlap,
you can still see
images of other lives.

like the one where i died,

where bliss never came.

VII. the idea of you

illusions brought me more
than you ever gave me.
i danced with the thought of something
even if it wasn't you
to compliment a longing
i could never endure.

VIII. torn (i,ii)

i.

i held the gun for you,
your hand in mine,
held it up to my chest
and blasted me away.

i'm torn without you.

ii.

i love you like a silenced gun.
                    without bullets, anyway.

41

IX. a knife without a blade

a year to let go
to pass us by
is a knife without a blade.

a year to miss and reminisce
drunken forlorn of lost hope
and bar-hops.

it doesn't matter much now.

a year to perceive our own reflection,

> creation
> addictions
> separation

the choices we've made —

> *madness!*

to punish with no comfort.
lovers without their other.

> *how much have you accomplished?*

in chaos,

> *have you found silence?*

and,
> *what is beautiful to you now?*

a year to go out,
to get it all out.

to do all the things i needed to do.
to purge whatever i've consumed.

a year...

> if we would have made it through.

X. my love

the look in your eyes still haunts me at night.

they wake me up from dreams that burn hot—burned
me,

whenever we'd get too close.

and yet,

despite the pain it brings,

i can't help but be drawn

to the fire

that burns.

XI. tortured

your cave gray eyes
fell outward.
your ears bled
and mouth spewed.

a demon in the dark
regurgitating
my hidden fears
and deepest desires.

he resists
            binding to denial.

i sing to your delusions and it hurts.
a requiem of peace
from the part of me
that wants to be free
            from you.

XII. inside

give me something
to unlock this box
to pry it open
to reveal what's inside.
break it down if we can.

i took a peak of its beauty to write you,
          after all.

XIII. (conversations) my love-hate relationship with love-hate

i love you.
i hate you.

you mean the world to me.
you mean nothing.

i would have given you the world.
i'll give myself my own fucking world.

i just want to be with you.
i'm not even sure that's true.

i can't get you out of my head.
you scarred me pretty badly.

i miss the way you smell.
it's just animal pheromones.

i accept you for who you are.
not the part that lies, obviously.

you write beautiful poetry.
most of what you say is bullshit.

i think you are gorgeous.
just before i remember your ugliness.

i want to give you my heart.
you shattered it the first time.

i think i'm in love with you.
only the thought of you.

i miss not having you in my life.

definitely for the best.

i learned so much from this experience.
i have so much regret.

i wish we could have been more honest and direct with
each other.
i was afraid and still am.

there is a first time for love.
this definitely was not it.

XIV. ghosts

the vows in your eyes
float like ghosts without a home.
you were never really there.

XV. humanness

i *wanted.*

that was my first mistake—

to feel human.
to get caught up in the world
and be vulnerable.
to love like i've never loved before
and
feel that love in return,
just before it'd get ugly.
just before you got ugly.

now,
that ugliness consumes.
it's part of the universal balance of things,
eating away at our very cores,
eating away at our everything.

      there is only *Nothing.*

      it's a cruel joke,

.   the nature of things.

CHAPTER 3
EPIPHANY

I. chaos meets bliss

godsent.
the universe engraved it
on my pillow
and on my wrist.
i'd kiss it
and would fall into heaven
right before
i'd float into hell.

i never thanked you
because i was too afraid
to feel that good
when all i knew
was the havoc
that i'd open my mouth to.

i never knew you—
but i'm getting to know me.

i thanked every piece of the throat
that broke you down,
that broke me down.

i thanked every spirit of rebellion
that drove you away
and sank right back into me.

i thanked every demon i felt i was
and every light she gave me
so that you, too,
could see things the way i do.

i thanked the ground for splitting in two
and holding a promise that one day
i could be just as beautiful
as you.

II. lack
as inspiration

i never faked it.
the universe just responded faster
to my sincerity
than you or i ever could have.

of all the things we have in common,
we know that pain makes the prettiest music.
tragic poetry like mine.
it's all a novel
that tears your heart up,
feeding on imaginary sorrows,
missing that kind of love.

i send thank you notes to the skies because i'm happy,
but i also can't write because of it.

creation,
inspiration—
to myself, at least,
only comes from longing.

true love makes me disappear,
but pain
brings me closer.

III. date night

teach me differently—
to love myself.
fly a kite with my name on it
to reach the highest heaven
just to show me
i can still make it.

IV. detach

i've given too many chances,
lived too many lives,
when you break off your arm
just to see it grow back.

V. sealed with a kiss

i made a choice that had to be done...

not because i didn't love you but because things were
going wrong and i couldn't go on with them.

      change needed to happen.

a healing process only time could take care of—

'mend-our-hearts' kind of time,

so,

that if one day,

we were to gaze into each other's eyes again,

it wouldn't be war we'd find,

but each other.

VI. manifest

how to create a muse
when yours has abandoned you?
how do you live in the same universe
as the one who's never known you?

VII. the pyre

a holy mountain of secret worship
for when the sun dies in the West,
        like an altar without a god
        or the Mona Lisa in a vault.

collapsing in on itself
        is the unborn child
breastfeeding on my lament,
wearing a halo as a martyr.
stroking it, is the Mother.

VIII. Aletheia

stir it all up
alpha-beta universe,
boiling beauty before it dies.

slowly simmering
at the perfect temperature,
long enough to melt the letters.

dropped my eye into the mixture
for clarity and heart.
add a taste
of my own being
to understand what it is
i'm eating.

manna from heaven,
all of nature in a bowl.
penciled in the weather
to make sure you come home.

sweet fragrance lingers
like a ghost that's always there.
awakening that hunger for truth,
while you're out at war.

we'll eat our creation
to end our starvation.

candles at the table,
one on each side.
a romantic dinner with hope and pain.
tears in our cups
to sprinkle as salt

for all the wisdom we've gained.
welcome Aletheia,
devour our brood.

i drink her wine 'til my cup is cleansed.
that will be the day
we make something new again.

IV. the last goodbye

i was reborn
from the stronghold of death
unto the depths of my being.
choosing to change for the better
so that nothing can be kept secret again
and there is no place for regret.

X. THIS, mirror

i never knew how much one could learn from a single
person...

it happens when you invest everything in them.
they wear a charming mask for you, one that's easy to fall
in love with...
convinces you of his infinite love, and vows to marry
you.
you love that mask because it makes you laugh and it
promises you the world,

    but eventually,

        it comes off,

and what's behind it is an unshakable fear—

and this fear moves you because you see it for what it is,
but it's so ugly, he can't even look at himself, and
gradually, he remembers why he hates his own
reflection.

it tears you up inside that they had this within all along,
and you keep taking them back because they shook your
whole foundation. they made you question love and
tested your faith.

they even made you cry as if mourning,

        which is significant to you.

    and they say they're changing.

    they say they're working it out.

you believe it because you never wanted to see them as anything less than perfect,

because you made a pact in each other's eyes that all the love you feel together, no matter how dysfunctional,

is perfect.

i trained myself just before meeting him that ugliness is beauty and there is no light without darkness.

so, i accepted him for who he is, naturally and effortlessly, and hoped he'd do the same for me.

unconditionally is how i loved.

every broken piece of him became my own until i realized he left me shattered...

and that is when i realized that there is no one there but myself and it's my own betrayal i've manifested... it was my own conditioning regarding love and beauty that

failed you / failed me.

a loss from the fear of losing each other.

and Pain—

Oh!

that sad, decrepit catalyst i adopted as my baby was our own consensual creation,

showing me i know nothing.
teaching me how not to be,

and reminding me
just how human i really am...

and I am thankful for it.

End of Conversations.

Preview

LVF.LVX's Upcoming Book

Excerpt from

Letters to Hadit:
Poems & Initiations

love me
as your Church,
the way i serve you
and exalt your glory
for all eternity.

About the Author

LVF.LVX is an enigmatic writer and artist with a deep love for the esoteric. As a brand and alter-ego, she is an obscurity, contradiction, and whatever you want her to be. She writes to transcend her sorrows, drawing from the ethereal for inspiration. When she's not writing, she enjoys dance, avant-garde art, and nature walks. With a degree in philosophy, her writing reflects a profound exploration of the human condition and relentless quest for truth— love being her greatest motivator. She invites you to join her on a series of initiations unveiling her truth, one poem at a time.

@LVF.LVX

Review Me on Amazon

Review Me on Good Reads

MallMagick.com